THE MAGIC OF SHRINKING WORRY

WRITTEN BY
ALLI S. KERT, PHD

Copyright ©2024 Alli Kert

All rights reserved. This book, or any portion thereof,
may not be reproduced in any form, without written
permission from the author or illustrator.

First Printing, 2024

Layout: Jessica Angerstein
ISBN: 979-8-89372-761-6

THIS BOOK IS DEDICATED TO

My family, and the families who trust me to work with theirs.

A little bit of worry
can be helpful.

Remember
to brush
your teeth
Don't forget
to do your
HOME WORK
Maybe I
should ask a
grown up
HELP
I should make
sure that's not
too hot

A **LOT** of worry is not helpful.

You'll NEVER be able to do that
Don't forget to check AGAIN
that's TOO HARD for you
what if I get it WRONG?

WORRY CAN TRICK US.

It's a tricky little fella!
It can make you think

that
you're in
trouble.

Or that
you can't
handle
stuff.

Or that
everything
is unsafe.

Worry worries
A LOT!

Worry should protect you.
It should NOT make you feel scared.

So what can you do?

LOTS
OF STUFF.

Turn the page, and
I'LL SHOW YOU HOW.

FIRST, YOU MUST LEARN WORRY'S TRICKS.

Worry likes to scare you.
It might make you ask grownups lots of
questions that start with "What if?"

That's just Worry's

Worry tries to trick you into thinking
you need to know all of the answers
to all the What-If? questions.

But those questions are **NOT** helpful!
You do not have to listen to Worry
or answer those What If? questions.

Worry pretends it can predict the future.
It warns you about all the bad stuff
that **MIGHT** happen, even when
those things probably **WON'T** happen!

That's just Worry's

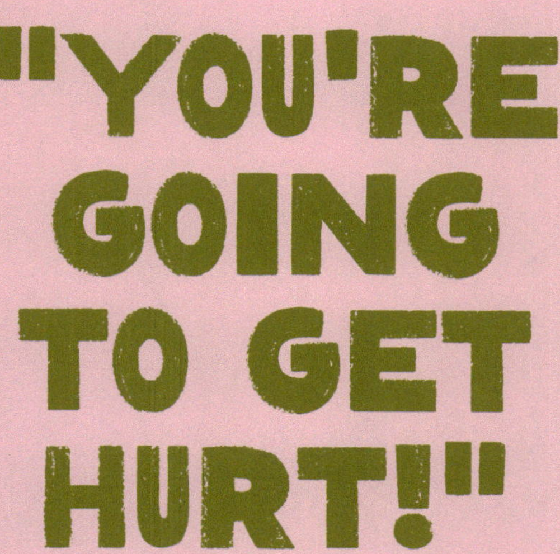

"YOU'RE GOING TO GET HURT!"

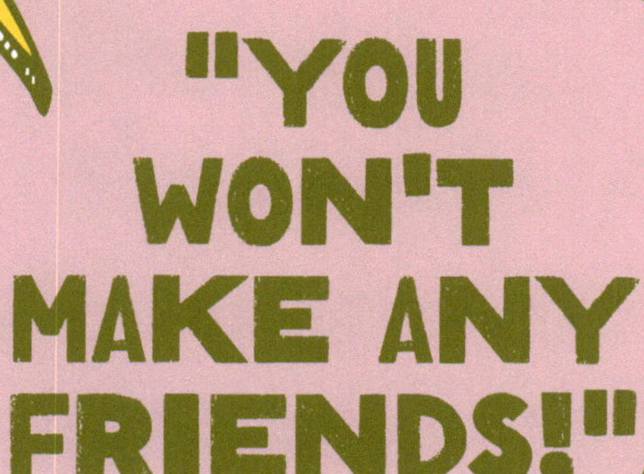

"YOU WON'T MAKE ANY FRIENDS!"

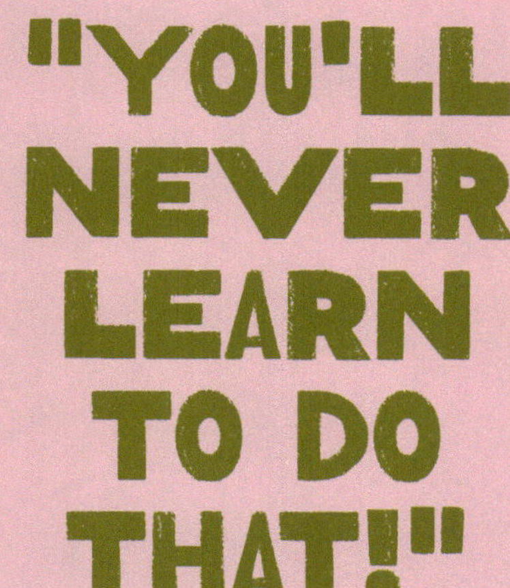

"YOU'LL NEVER LEARN TO DO THAT!"

Worry likes to make you believe that if what you're worried about *does* happen, it'll be...

That's just Worry's

Good news, though.
Worry often **LIES** about
how bad things **could** be.

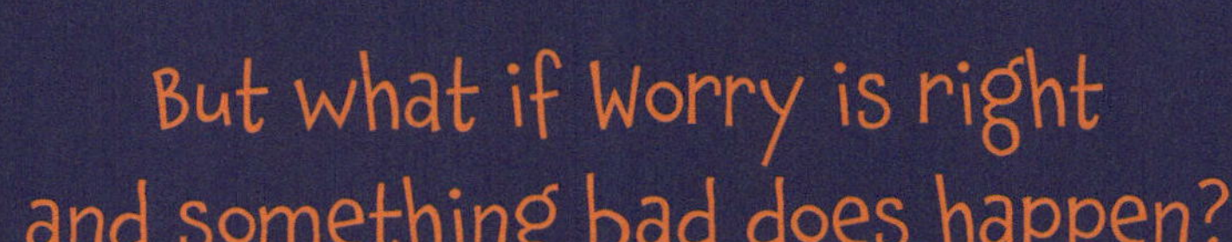

But what if Worry is right
and something bad does happen?

That's just Worry's

But you **WILL** be okay.
Whatever you're worried about might be hard.
It might be really hard.
It might even be really, really bad.

BUT...

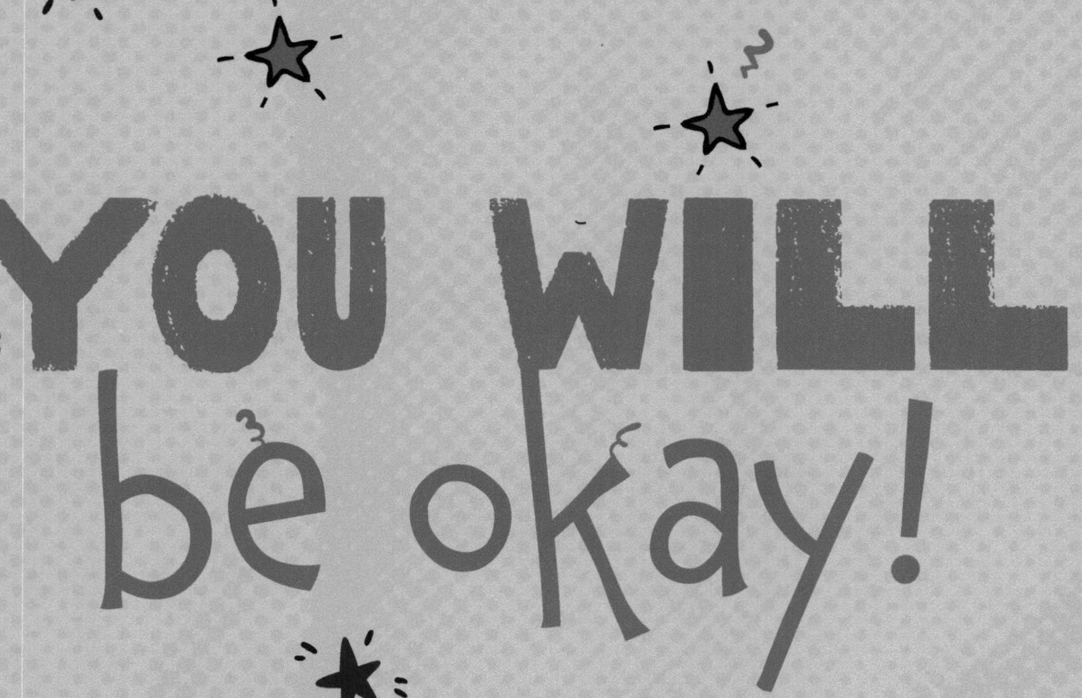
YOU WILL
be okay!

There's some simple stuff you can do to help you feel better. It involves

A **LITTLE**

MAGIC.

ARE YOU READY
FOR IT?

Now that you can spot Worry's tricks,
it's time to learn your magic tricks.

You can learn the **MAGIC**
of shrinking Worry.

That's right, you can shrink a
big Worry into a wee Worry - or
even make it completely disappear.

POOf

LIKE
MAGIC

YOU CAN DO IT,
AND I'LL SHOW YOU HOW.

The first trick is talking to a grown-up about your Worry.

I bet there's one near you right now.

Did you know that parents and teachers worry too?

It can be hard to talk about your Worry.

But remember, you can handle anything!

The grown-up might understand
why you're feeling worried.
Maybe they worried about the same thing
when they were your age.

Sometimes, talking about a worry helps it
shrink from a big Worry to a wee Worry -

Now you know that you can handle
even the **BIGGEST** worry.

Can you think of all the things MORE
likely to happen than the bad stuff
Worry is telling you will happen?

How about spending a few minutes
thinking about what will happen
if things DO work out? Hmm...

AND NOW YOU HAVE YOUR OWN!

I bet that sounds pretty good.
BECAUSE THAT, RIGHT THERE,

Ready for another magic trick
to shrink Worry?

You can remind yourself of other worries you've had.
I bet you've had other **BIG** worries
that you've magically shrunk into wee worries.

You've gone through some really hard stuff.
And here you are.

YOU REALLY CAN HANDLE ANYTHING!

You were okay then,
and you will be okay now!

Maybe you're worried about something
you're going to do in the future,
like going to a new school, learning to swim,
or attending a birthday party.

Do you want to know another magic trick to shrink Worry?
It's an easy one. Are you ready? Okay, here it is...

JUST ·DO· IT

That's right. Do whatever it is that
you're worried about doing.
I bet you'll shrink Worry.
If you do it again, you might even
forget all about that Worry.

There's that **MAGIC** again!

You are in charge of your worries.

YES, YOU!

Sometimes Worries become so small that
you hardly know they're there.
Sometimes they might even
disappear completely.

poof
LIKE MAGIC

Last, remember what you read on page 21?
No? Go on, flip back to see.

That's right, no matter what happens,
no matter how bad it seems,

YOU WILL be okay...ALWAYS!

Shrinking Worries takes practice.

The more you practice the better you get at
turning big Worries into wee Worries.

It might help to read this book a bunch of times.
Remember, no matter what happens and
no matter how bad it seems...

Here's a list of Worries tricks ⚠️
to help you spot them if they pop up:

Here's a checklist of the magic tricks
YOU can use to help shrink worry

PAGE 26 — Talk to a grown-up.

PAGE 29 — Think about what things will be like if they work out.

PAGE 32 — Recall other worries you've had that you've made disappear.

PAGE 34 — **JUST DO IT!**

PAGE 38 — Remember, you WILL be okay!

ABOUT THE AUTHOR

DR. ALLI KERT is a NYS licensed psychologist and certified school psychologist who partners with parents and children to improve quality of life through simplification, understanding and consistency. Dr. Kert specializes in helping children and their caregivers to understand and manage anxiety. She lives and works on the Upper East Side of Manhattan with her husband and boys.

www.ingramcontent.com/pod-product-compliance
Lightning Source LLC
Chambersburg PA
CBHW042002110726

48006CB00004B/964

9 798889 372761